Ophelia:

"There's fennel for you, and columbines. There's rue for you, and here's some for me. We may call it herb of grace o' Sundays. O, you must wear your rue with a difference! There's a daisy. I would give you some violets but they withered all when my father died. They say he made a good end." HAMLET IV: V: 179-186 (The Riverside Shakespeare 1974)

A Complete List of Works by This Author:

https://www.amazon.com/author/anniswardjackson

OPHELIA'S SATIRICAL DIADEM

DIADEM

Herbs in Shakespeare's HAMLET

Annis Ward Jackson

OPHELIA'S SATIRICAL DIADEM
Herbs in Shakespeare's HAMLET

Copyright 2009 by Annis Ward Jackson

SunnyBrick Publishers

Acknowledgements:

I owe my gratitude to many people along the way, my mother who fostered my interest in words and reading, many excellent teachers, especially Dr. F. David Sanders who was director of the honors program and my adviser at East Carolina University.

I am especially grateful to my husband whose support has been essential and absolute in all my writing ventures.

Contents

PURPOSE

The intention of this work is to show the relationship of the herbs in Shakespeare's Hamlet to the passages of the play in which they appear, and more specifically, the herb's relationship to each character with which they are associated.

A history of herbs and herbals begins this work, and is followed by a chapter on garden imagery and two herbs that are associated only with Hamlet.

Chapter three discusses the remainder of the herbs in the play, both those that Ophelia hands to Claudius, Gertrude, and Laertes, and those that she weaves into her fantastic garland.

The aim of this study was to present both the literary and the traditional lore of each herb with the main focus on finding a common thread that would link them within Hamlet, the play. That thread is a concern with things sexual, and specifically, sexual corruption.

Each herb mentioned, however briefly, has a history of being used as an aphrodisiac, an anti-aphrodisiac, a cure for venereal disease, or has some other interrelated sexual association.

INTRODUCTION

"Herb" is first defined in the Oxford English Dictionary as a soft-stemmed plant that dies to the ground or completely dies after flowering. The more specific definition based on use is stated in the OED "as applied to plants of which the leaves, or stems and leaves, are used for food or medicine, or in some way for their scent or flavor" (230).

My earliest memory of myself is at the age of three, playing in the shade of an oak tree while my parents gathered Witch Hazel leaves in a nearby field. Too young to be of help then, I would later join them and my older brothers for long days in the fields and woods in the Appalachian Mountains of North Carolina gathering all manner of roots and herbs for sale to Wilcox Drug Company in Boone, North Carolina. My maternal grandmother who made numerous medicines from plants gathered in the wild and others from her garden, added to my early association with herbs.

As an adult I never lost interest in the fascinating world of herbs. Along the way I began to grow a wide selection of both wild and domestic varieties. My interest in herbs was equaled only by a lifetime love of literature, especially the works of William Shakespeare.

Therefore, it was only natural that I became increasingly aware of the emphasis he put on nature, plants especially, in his plays. Many of the plants that appear in Shakespeare's works are, to the novice, only flowers. The herb enthusiast knows, however, that violets, pansies, lilies, and many other so-called flowers have been used for medicinal as well as other purposes for many centuries.

This work is by no means a complete study of the herbs in Shakespeare. A volume of encyclopedic proportions would be required to present research on each plant and show where each appears in the plays, poems, and sonnets. Analyzing passages where each plant appears and supplying critical distinctions for its appearance in those passages would fill another volume.

Therefore, I concentrate only on the herbs in Hamlet. Other plays contain more references to herbs than Hamlet but my choice is the result of a strong fascination with Ophelia's "fantastic garland" and with the mysterious poison that killed Old Hamlet.

My objective is to show that these and other herbs in Hamlet share qualities that accentuate the gross corruption of the court of Denmark. I give evidence that Shakespeare was well informed about those qualities and the folklore surrounding the herbs he used in Hamlet, that he was aware of his audience's knowledge of those herbs, and that he used the herbs to elucidate those passages in which they appear.

To gather historical information on the herbs in Hamlet, I consider it necessary to refer to all potentially relevant sources. Consequently, a short history of early sources was needed to give the reader some indication of the importance of herbs to humankind over thousands of years.

My intention in this area is to show the amount of knowledge of herbs that was available to Shakespeare's audience in both written and oral form. In order to see the relevance of more recent evidence, attention must be paid to the commentaries from the nineteenth and twentieth centuries that explore the plants and/or gardens in Shakespeare's works. The short history and the commentaries are presented in chapter one, along with a discussion of the herbal that the poet most likely consulted.

Chapter two deals with garden imagery in Shakespeare's works and with the two herbs that are not directly associated with Ophelia: savory and wormwood.

Chapter three deals with the herbs that are directly related to Ophelia.

I feel fortunate that my association with herbs allows me to choose a topic that is of interest not only to those with an appreciation of great literature but also to a broad spectrum of society today. I offer in my bibliography evidence for this assertion.

Since I currently cultivate a majority of the herbs that appear in Hamlet, descriptions of shape, color, fragrance, and taste are derived from my own experience.

For those herbs with which I do not have personal experience, I have relied on authoritative sources from the ancient Greeks through the twentieth century.

SECTION ONE

Herbals and Treatments

A. Herbs in Historical Perspective

For as long as mankind has existed, human beings have maintained a relationship with plants unlike their relationship with any other entity. Plants provided early man with a confirmation that life was a cycle, that rebirth was possible. Humans could watch plants come to life in the spring, grow, bear fruit, and die back in the fall, only to reappear the next spring. Perhaps by chance humans discovered that plants not only provided food but that they helped to cure illness, heal wounds, or alter the mind in such a way as to put them in close contact with the gods or other worlds.

In Patterns in Comparative Religions, Mercia Eliade discusses at length the theory of archetypal vegetation in the development of the most ancient cultures: "No plant is of value in itself; its value is in its relationship to an archetype, or in the repeating of a set of actions or words which make the plant sacred by setting it apart from its profane surroundings." Eliade goes on to illustrate this idea by discussing "two ancient incantations in the sixteenth century which accompanied the gathering of herbs with healing powers" (296).

Very early man formed a unique union with plants, which can be substantiated even before the existence of a language. Some 60,000 years ago a Neanderthal man was buried in a cave in Iraq. When the grave was opened in 1960, archaeologists found large amounts of pollen surrounding the human remains.

The pollen was scientifically examined and was determined to have come from eight different plants, all of which can be found growing today in the fields and woods of Iraq. Seven of the eight species continue to be used by the local people for medicine. Experts in the field speculate that the corpse was that of a great leader or a Shaman or medicine man, since evidence from later cultures points toward the practice of placing in the grave items that are valuable or which will help the deceased into the other world (Soleki 880-81).

The history of civilized man's use of plants as herbs is well documented from the very beginning in various forms. One of the earliest herbals was written around 2800 BC by a Chinese herbalist, Shen Nung, who also happened to be an emperor. In Pen T'ao Kang-Mu, Shen Nung listed 366 medicinal plants and 8,160 prescriptions (Bunney 9).

In the eighteenth century BC, the Code of Hammurabi included among the rules that governed almost every facet of Babylonian life, many references to healing plants. Varieties of common mints, henbane, Hyoscyamus niger, and licorice, Glycyrrhiza are referred to throughout the Code (Griggs 10).

The great Hippocrates (460-477 BC), whose oath is still taken by physicians, was an accomplished herbalist who believed in what came to be known in the Middle Ages as the Doctrine of Signatures. This belief held that the shape and appearance of an herb determined the disease it was intended to cure (Bunney 10).

Aristotle's successor Theophrastus (372-387 BC) wrote The History of Plants, for which he is called the "father of botany." In the ninth book of The History of Plants Theophrastus summarized all the Greeks knew about the medicinal properties of plants (Durant 2:637-38).

All of the above writings can be called herbals of sorts. However, the first true herbal came into being around the first century AD. Rodale's Illustrated Encyclopedia Of Herbs defines an herbal as a book written for laypersons which describes plants and tells how to use them. "In an age when both books and doctors tended to be rare and expensive, the herbal held a valued place in every literate household" (Kowalchik 32).

In the first century AD, a Sicilian army surgeon, Pedanius Dioscorides, compiled a great herbal De Materia Medica in his native Greek. Unlike its eclectic predecessors De Materia Medica was a true herbal. Dioscorides took a pragmatic approach to plants. If they were not useful for food and medicine, he simply disregarded them (Anderson 7-8). An examination of the modern copy of Dioscorides' herbal as translated into English by John Goodyer in 1655, however, gives the impression that all plants have some useful purpose.

In the same century in which Dioscorides lived and wrote, Pliny the Elder (AD 23-79), a Roman statesman, wrote Naturalis Historia. Books XII-XVII comprise an herbal that became a major source for herbalists in the Middle Ages (Anderson 16-18). Claudius Galen (AD 121-200), a physician from Asia Minor who became the personal medical attendant to Marcus Aurelius, compiled Peri Krateos kai dunameos ton naplon pharmakon, in which he evaluated all drug plants in terms of their relation to the doctrine of the four humors: yellow bile, black bile, blood, and phlegm (Griggs 14-15). In the early fifth century AD, a man called Apicius compiled De Re Coquinaria, an herbal cookbook. The book is filled with recipes calling for all manner of herbs to season and tenderize, and also to camouflage the odor of tainted meats (Edwards lx-xl).

While herbal knowledge was being disseminated by way of printed matter, Roman armies were spreading the actual herbs throughout Europe and Great Britain. The legions traveled with their own doctors and carried with them supplies of the most used herbs. Physic gardens were frequently planted near Roman encampments in order that herbs such as the Madonna lily, Lilium candidum, could be at hand for dressing the wounds of soldiers (Griggs 13).

However, long before the Romans filtered across Europe and into Great Britain, the British Isles had substantial knowledge of plants used for healing, seasoning, and fumigating. Pliny the Elder commented on the Celts' use of mistletoe in religious ceremonies and as a medicine (Grigson 201).

Early in the sixth century AD, St. Benedict issued his Rules for the Benedictine monasteries of Europe. In chapter 36, he entreats his brethren to take care of the sick in a special room in the monastery (McCann 43). When Christianity was carried into England around AD 597, the vast knowledge of herbal properties that had been gathered and maintained by the monasteries of Europe came with the new religion. This knowledge was preserved by Benedictine monks in England and Ireland and was later returned to war-ravaged Europe (Griggs 19).

Evidence of the continuing importance of herbs during the Middle Ages is apparent upon examination of the Plan of St. Gall, an architectural design for a Benedictine monastery that never came to fruition. The plan, dated AD 820, calls for both a medicinal herb garden and a kitchen garden with herbs used for enhancing the monk's mostly vegetarian diet. The names of herbs to be grown in each garden are specifically listed in the architectural plan (Horn & Born 203-209).

Hildegarde of Bingen, an abbess and mystic wrote Physica, an important and very useful herbal around 1150. The earliest book on natural history to be written in German, its sections on herbs greatly influenced many sixteenth century herbalists (Anderson 51-58).

Few herbals were written during the thirteenth and fourteenth centuries, but during the fifteenth century, with the invention of movable type printing, books became cheaper and more plentiful. Literacy increased and book-culture became a basic part of the European way of life. The first Latin editions of Dioscorides' De Materia Medica and Theophrastus' The History of Plants were printed in the late fifteenth century (Arber 272). Hortus Sanitatus was translated into the Latin in 1501. The remaining years of the fifteenth century through the mid-seventeenth century can be truly called the "age of herbals." The era opened in Germany in the mid-sixteenth century with works by Otto Brunfels and Leonard Fuchs, two equally acclaimed fathers of German botany. Brunfels' and Fuchs' works are still unsurpassed in the quality of their illustrations of herbs. A Belgian, Rembert Dodoens, published Cruydeboeck in 1554. Other noted herbals were published in France, Switzerland, Italy, Spain, and Portugal (Arber 52-68).

Bankes Herball was the earliest book of a botanical nature printed in English. Published in 1525, the herbal was both popular and valuable for its emphasis on botanical information and for its poetic style (Arber 41-42). However, the importance of Bankes Herball was surpassed in 1526 when Peter Treveris translated from French to English The Grete Herball (Arber 44-51). In 1551, a Fellow at Pembroke College, Cambridge University, William Turner completed his work The New Herball, of which Frank Anderson says,

"English botany can be properly be said to begin with the herbal of William Turner" (148).

The three herbals best known in modern times were published during the Renaissance: John Gerard's The Herball or Historie of Plants (1797), John Parkinson's Paridisi In Sol Paradisus Terrestros (1629), and Nicholas Culpeper's Complete Herball (1653). Lesser known today is The Nieeve Herball, a 1578 translation by Henry Lyte of Dodoens' Cruydeboeck.

Like books of a botanical nature, publications comparable to twentieth-century "how-to" books were popular in the Renaissance. Thomas Hill's A Most Brief and Pleasant Treatise, Teaching How to Dress, Sowe, and Set a Garden (1563) and Peter Loven's The Pathway to Health (1582) are good examples of books of instructions that explore to some extent the common use of herbs. The English Housewife (1615), by Gervase Markham, shows just how important those plants commonly called herbs were to everyday life in the Renaissance. The book is filled with detailed instructions on how to be a proper housewife. Chapter three is devoted entirely to the art of distillery wherein the housewife learned to make perfumes, medicines, and flavorings with the aid of a still that is very similar to the "moonshine still" of the twentieth century. The "stillroom" that is mentioned frequently in Renaissance literature is where this handiwork took place. Other sections of The English Housewife contain instructions on growing and harvesting a wide variety of herbs, and on how to use them for medicines, seasonings, foods, perfumes, and flavorings. Michael Best, editor of McGill-Queen's 1986 edition of The English Housewife, calls the book "the most comprehensive, the most practiced, and the most readable of the many books of instruction written for women in the early seventeenth century" (Markham ix).

Although the notion has been debated in recent years, the number of "how-to" books published in Renaissance England suggests a relatively literate populace. Alfred Harbage, in Shakespeare's Audience, offers his view of the English population in general: "It seems probable that the rank and file were more literate in the sixteenth century than in the eighteenth" (146). Harbage cites J.W. Adamson's study in which Adamson concluded, "The people of London constituted 'by no means an illiterate society'" (146). However, the level of literacy is not the only relevant issue. We must assume that some of the written knowledge of herbs trickled down to the lower classes and merged with the massive amount of traditional knowledge that had been a part of their culture for centuries.

Harbage believes that Shakespeare wrote for his audience (51), and that craftsmen made up much of that audience: "Many were highly skilled, performing functions now allotted to the chemist, architect, and engineer: (68). Obviously, the operative word for our purposes here is "chemist." This suggests a populace that relied on its own class to make medicines, potions, or perfume from available sources that were most commonly herbs.

Given the number of huge volumes written on herbs in the Renaissance, one may rightly conclude that William

Shakespeare did not fail to put to advantage this knowledge he shared with his theater patrons. At once literary and traditional, the knowledge would have prepared an audience well for the artful and subtle way in which the leading playwright of the day referred to herbs in his works.

B. Modern Treatment of Herbs in Shakespeare

Books that explore Shakespeare's references to herbs comprise a long list. I have personally examined those by Beisley, Bloom, Dent, Ellacombe, Grindon, Savage, Seager, Singleton, and Thiselton-Dyer. Almost without exception, these books are catalogues that tell where the plant appears in Shakespeare's works and then give a short statement on the most common knowledge about the plant.

Beisley, in some instances, does attempt to align the lore of the plant with the scene in which it appears. Thiselton-Dyer stops short of literary interpretation as related to the plant lore and tends to quote Ellacombe and Beisley for general information instead of going to primary sources. All of these works stay with "safe" interpretations and seldom elaborate on sexual or other possibly controversial connotations of the herbs.

It is evident, however, from statements in the introductions of some of these works, that the authors, themselves obviously very knowledgeable about plants, agree that Shakespeare maintained a special relationship with plants and gardening. Beisley says that Shakespeare's "knowledge of botany was not less than that of any other branch of natural history he investigated and described" (xviii).

Leo Grindon agrees: "What Shakspere has done for us botanically, and in this respect so excellently, is found in sweeter and more loving and more copious mention of plants and flowers than occurs in any other single writer. Comparing Shakspere with other poetic literature in respect to a profusion of reference to trees and plants, he is surpassed only by the Old Testament writers" (3-4)

Ellacombe offers an even more glowing statement after concluding that Shakespeare was neither a professed gardener nor, in a scientific sense, a botanist. "His knowledge of plants was simply the knowledge that every man may have who goes through the world with his eyes open to the beauties of Nature that surround him" (1).

Ellacombe also is convinced and declares that Shakespeare never mentions a plant unnecessarily: "When he names a plant or flower, he does it not to show his knowledge, but because the particular flower or plant is wanted in the particular place in which he uses it" (3). If this statement can be substantiated, there exists an important and exciting area of Shakespeare's works that has been virtually unexplored!

Thiselton-Dyer begins his section on plants in Shakespeare by saying, "That Shakespeare possessed an extensive knowledge of the history and superstition associated with flowers is evident from only a slight perusal of his plays." He goes on to say that Shakespeare has, with a master's hand, "interwoven many a little legend or superstition, thereby infusing an additional force to his writing" (86).

Caroline Spurgeon goes one step beyond the use of single flowers or herbs. "One occupation, one point of view, above all others, is naturally his, that of a gardener. All through his plays he thinks most easily and readily of human life and action in terms of a gardener" (86).

If however, as Ellacombe contends, Shakespeare was not a professed gardener, nor a botanist, then from where came his knowledge of plants and how they grow, their usages, and their lore? Ellacombe conjectures that Shakespeare most likely knew John Gerard personally and that they must have known each other's works (4). Spurgeon points out: "The most common running metaphor and picture in Shakespeare's mind in the early historical plays as a whole (from I Henry VI to Richard II inclusive) is that of growth as seen in a garden and orchard" (216).

The early dates of these plays, ca. 1581-1598, (Evans 48-50) make unlikely Shakespeare's use of Gerard's printed Herbal (1597) as a direct source. However, there is a strong possibility that Shakespeare saw the manuscript or that he gained knowledge about gardening, and herbs in particular, from John Gerard, the man.

A stronger possibility is that the poet consulted Henry Lyte's translation, The Nievve Herbal (1578). F.D. and F.F.M. Hoeniger state emphatically that if Shakespeare was familiar with any specific herbal, it was Lyte's. Their most compelling evidence is that Lyte's herbal was printed many times over and was "deservedly the most popular herbal in England during the last two decades of the sixteenth century (55).

In Middle-Class Culture of Elizabethan England, L.B. Wright says in comparing several herbals, "the reading public preferred Lyte's translation which gave more botany along with its remedies and recipes (576). Frank Anderson also strongly suggests Lyte's herbal as the one that Shakespeare would most likely have used (178).

In her comprehensive history Herbals, Their Origin and Evolution, Agnes Arber regrettably does not address the question of which herbal Shakespeare might have used, but she directly connects The Nievve Herbal, in Lyte's translation, to one of Shakespeare's contemporaries, Edmund Spenser. Arber says that in the Aprill eclogue of Spenser's Shepheardes Calendar, "five flowers that Spenser first mentions occur within sixteen pages" of Lyte's herbal.

Lady Mary Herbert, a close friend of Spenser's, lived near Lyte and was a confirmed flower lover. "It thus seems not unlikely that she would have acquired a copy of the herbal, and that it might have been shown to Spenser" (127).

This is by no means proof that Shakespeare consulted Lyte's translation, but we may be safe in assuming the possibility, as Anderson and Hoeniger suggest. Just as writers today consult such texts as Roget's Thesaurus or Fowler's Modern English Usage, so might Henry Lyte's The Nievve Herbal have filled that niche in Shakespeare's day.

SECTION TWO

The Unweeded Garden, Satyrs, and Hebona

A. Garden Imagery

Shakspere's Garden (1864) by Sidney Beisley, Shakespeare's Garden (1903) by J. Harvey Bloom, and The Shakespeare Garden (1922) by Esther Singleton, are examples of the many volumes that have been devoted to the "Shakespeare's Garden" conversation since the seventeenth century. However, these books, and most others like them have very little to say about garden imagery. Instead, they are devoted to a literal garden that Shakespeare might have had, or a "suppose" garden patterned after the elaborate Elizabethan knot gardens that appear in the poet's works. This focus on a literal garden is interesting but it does nothing to explore or explain the significant use of garden imagery in Shakespeare's plays.

Garden imagery is common in literary works of the sixteenth and seventeenth centuries and in most cases a sexual theme is dominant. One has only to examine such works as Spenser's Faerie Queen (1589), Thomas Campion's "There is a Garden in her Face" (1617), and Andrew Marvell's "The Mower Against Gardens" (1681). Arlene Okerland describes the garden in Spenser's "Bower of Bliss" as a place dedicated to the pursuit of intemperate lust and calls the garden a giant sexual metaphor where everything within it entices humans toward their natural impulses (62-68). Thomas Campion's poem clearly represents a female preserving her virginity until the appropriate time. Andrew Marvell speaks of "luxurious man" in the first line of "Mower Against Gardens." The words luxurious, lecherous, lascivious, and unchaste were synonyms to Marvell and his contemporaries (OED 520).

Certainly no more than a "slight perusal" of Shakespeare's works in needed to show that he used his knowledge of gardening to construct clever and fitting analogies and images. In Henry VIII 3.2, Cardinal Wolsey compares his fall from grace to plants killed by frost:

This is the state of man: today he puts forth
The tender leaves of hopes, tomorrow blossoms,
And bears its blushing honor thick upon him;
The third day comes a frost, a killing frost, (252-355)[1]

---

[1]   All quotations are from The Riverside Shakespeare, G. Blakemore Evans (Boston: Houghton Mifflin, 1974).

One of the most obvious examples of gardening imagery is in Othello, where Iago compares men and their vices and virtues to gardens, "Virtue? A fig! 'tis in ourselves that we are thus or thus. Our bodies are our gardens, to the which our wills are gardeners" (1.3.319-21).

Perhaps the best-known garden image is in Richard II. Indeed, this image presents the whole of England as a garden.

> When our sea-walled garden, the whole land,
> Is full of weeds, her fairest flowers chok'd up,
> Her fruit trees all unprun'd, her hedges ruined,
> Her knots disordered, and her wholesome herbs
> Swarming with caterpillars? (3.4.43-47).

In Hamlet, Shakespeare paints a picture of a garden that is not merely unkempt from neglect and in danger from the elements, but a garden that is overtaken by "things rank and gross." This image of a neglected and diseased garden appears early in the play. When Hamlet, in his first soliloquy, laments the Church's position on "self-slaughter," he vents his grief by likening it to a garden: "Fie on't, oh fie! 'tis an unweeded garden / That grows to seed, things rank and gross in nature / possess it merely" (1.2.135-37).

Later when the Ghost begins to tell Hamlet the story of his death, he gains Hamlet's attention by telling him that if Hamlet does not act upon the story he is about to hear, he must be duller "than the fat weed / That roost itself on Lethe wharf" (1.5.32-33). "Lethe," according to the OED, is a river in Hades that produces lethargy and forgetfulness (217). The image here is one that foreshadows Hamlet's "dull revenge," "to sleep and eat, " "bestial oblivion," and neglect of "honor" in act four, scene four (Jenkins 455). The Ghost goes on to say that the crime against him occurred "while sleeping in my orchard" (1.5.35 and 59). In Renaissance literature "orchard" is synonymous with "garden" (Jenkins 217). In that garden, relates the Ghost, he was "cut off even in the blossom of my sin" (1.5.76).

In the nunnery scene, Hamlet uses a metaphor from the ancient horticultural practice of grafting in which a portion of one plant is attached to another. That portion grows and becomes a part of its host but remains a separate species bearing its own fruit. Hamlet says that "virtue cannot be so inoculate our old stock but we shall have relish of it" (3.1.117-18). In other words, "A graft of virtue cannot so change our original sinful nature that we shall not still have the flavor of it" (Jenkins 282).

Laertes, in warning Ophelia against Hamlet's attentions, uses the image of flowers assaulted by a worm or a disease: "The canker galls the infants of spring / Too oft before their buttons be disclos'd" (1.3.39-40). Laertes later refers to Ophelia as a "Rose of May" (4.5.157). His reference occurs after he learns that she has gone mad, that a "young maid's wits / should be as mortal as an old man's life" (4.5.160-61), that his blossoming sister has been destroyed before she has had an opportunity to come to full bloom.

The untended, overgrown, and diseased garden in which a young man contemplates suicide, a young maid loses her mind and does commit suicide, and political and sexual corruption is rampant, is filled with an array of herbs that fits the image perfectly. Strong evidence points to the herbs having been chosen specifically for their association with "things rank and gross."

B. Savory

Satureja montana, winter savory, is a shrubby perennial with slim dark evergreen leaves. Small white to lavender flowers usually appear in late summer. Satureja hortensis is summer savory. The main difference in the two is in their cultivation. The summer variety is an annual and must be reseeded each spring. Today the primary use of the two savories is culinary. They are popular as a substitute for sage in hardy soups and pork stuffing. They are especially good in recipes calling for wild game.

Hamlet uses the word savory in one of his speeches to the players: "I remember one said there were no sallets in the / lines to make the matter savory" (2.2.441-42). This is an example of an herb, the properties of which had become so well known that the name was, and is, a common adjective to mean "spicy or zesty" (OED 142). Therefore, Hamlet is saying that there were no "hot" lines in the play. Both winter and summer savory were popular in England in Shakespeare's day. Culpeper says that both varieties of the herb were "so well know that (being entertained as constant inhabitants in our gardens) they need no description." He gives many medicinal uses for the savories including the treatment of coughs, migraines, sciatica, gout, and warts (166).

The savories are directly associated with lechery. Bankes Herbal says of savory, "It is hot and dry in the third degree; therefore it is burning and stirreth him that useth lechery, therefore it is forbidden to use it much in meat" (83). The Latin Satureja signifies that in ancient Greece the herb belonged to the Satyrs, the lecherous goat-men of Greek mythology (Grieve 718-19). Hamlet has called Claudius satyr in comparison to his father, the Hyperion, or sun-god (1.2.140). When Hamlet uses the word savory, he is in the process of staging a drama that will reveal what he considers the lust and lechery in Claudius' marriage to Gertrude.

C. Wormwood

Wormwood, Artemisia absinthium is a shrubby perennial that has finely cut silver-green foliage. Large sprays of brownish yellow flower buds appear in late summer. Wormwood has been used over the centuries for the ailment from whence comes its common name, worms, especially stomach worms in children. A tea made from steeping the leaves in hot water was given as a spring tonic and de-wormer as late as the early twentieth century. Wormwood has remained popular as a moth repellent and can still be purchased in the form of sachets to hang among one's clothing.

Wormwood, the herb that is synonymous with bitterness, appears four times in the entire works of Shakespeare. In Romeo and Juliet, the nurse speaks of putting wormwood on her nipples in order to wean the child Juliet (1.3.26, 30). Rosaline uses wormwood as an adjective to describe Lord Berowne's satirical wit in Love's Labor's Lost (4.2.847). In "The Rape of Lucrece," "bitter wormwood taste" speaks for itself ((893). Hamlet says in an aside, "That's wormwood!" (3.2.181).

It has been generally assumed that Hamlet's intent is to specify bitterness when he mentions the herb in response to the Player Queen's description of the death of her husband. I believe that Hamlet was naming the poison that killed his father, Old Hamlet, instead of saying simply, "That's bitter!"

To make even a weak case for this suggestion, we must return to act one, scene five, where the Ghost is telling Hamlet the circumstances of his death. "Cursed Hebona" was poured into Old Hamlet's ears. The "leprous distilment" coursed through his body, curdling his blood and causing a "tetter," (a pustular herpetiform eruption of the skin, OED 235), "with vile and loathsome crust" to cover "all my smooth body" (1.5.62-73).

Over the centuries scholars have made varying suggestions about the identity of "hebona."   A. L. Rowse suggests henbane (1745), Dover Wilson also says henbane (292), Beisley says hemlock (4 Grindon chooses the Yew tree (46-47), and based solely on the pronunciation of "hebona," Singer proposes ebony (28). Each of these scholars fails to explain the poison beyond the possibility of its name as a corruption of hemlock, henbane, or ebony. Therefore, we need to find an herb that would not only fit the sound of hebenon or hebona, but also fit the horrible symptoms of Old Hamlet's death.

None of the former suggestions is one that cannot be logically and sensibly refuted. Ebony, a hard black wood, is not in any form regarded as a poison (Jenkins 456). The suggestion that the toxin that killed Old Hamlet was derived from the Yew tree is based purely on speculation. Taxus baccatta produces an alkaloid poisoning, which would cause none of Old Hamlet's symptoms before death. Christopher Marlowe refers to "the juice of hebon" as a poison in The Jew of Malta (298). Henry Bradley says that Marlowe misunderstands Gower's quotation from Ovid's Metamorphoses, where Ovid refers to hebenus as a "sleepy tree" (85-87). The yew was among a number of trees that early writers seemed to have referred to as "hebenus" (86).

Hemlock, Conium maculatum, has been well known as a poison since it was used to execute Socrates in 399 BC. All parts of the plant are poisonous, especially the ripened seeds (Bunney 116). Death of the victim is brought on almost immediately as the poison causes complete paralysis and asphyxia (Grieve 393). However, there is no evidence to show that hemlock is fatal if absorbed through the skin.

Henbane, Hyoscyamus niger, is not indigenous to Great Britain but by the sixteenth century had already been cultivated there for many years. Henbane's toxic properties are alkaloids, like the Yew tree, that attack the central nervous system (Bunney). Henry Lyte says of henbane: "The juice of the leaves and greene stalks {distilled with water} is good against paine in the ears" (321). Culpeper wrote, "The oil of the seed and juice of the herb or root is helpful for deafness, noise, and worms in the ears, being dropped therein" (92).

Would Shakespeare have used, for such a death as constitutes the very basis of his play, a poison commonly known as a soothing remedy for an earache? Would he even have used a poison that had no reputation for being absorbed through the skin?

Where then are we to look for the answer? Does it matter whether we know the specific poison that killed Old Hamlet? The answer must be both, yes and no. No, it would not make a real difference in the way we look at the play. No, it would not change any important part of the plot. Old Hamlet is dead and cannot be any more or less dead because we may be able to say specifically what poison was used to murder him. However, in another sense, yes, it does matter. Any question matters so long as we can make even one word less ambiguous or one action more clear. Harold Jenkins suggests that it is a mistake to try to equate hebona with any real plant (457). I would agree that efforts to equate hebona with any plant outside the play have been unproductive. It is within the play that an herb is mentioned, an herb surrounded by truth and lore that at least suggests that it is worthy of being considered in the search for the poison that killed Hamlet's father. When Hamlet says, "That's wormwood" (3.2.181), does he mean that the Player Queen's speech is bitter, or does he mean that wormwood is the poison that killed his father?

As mentioned above, Shakespeare does use wormwood to mean bitter in varying senses elsewhere in his works. However, it is perfectly clear in each of those instances that wormwood means literally bitter. Hamlet does not speak of "wormwood taste" literally as in Romeo and Juliet, nor metaphorically as in Love's Labor's Lost. Instead, in response to the Player Queen's lament, "In second husband let me be accurs'd / None wed the second but who killed the first" (3.2.179-80), Hamlet says in an aside, "That's wormwood." Shakespeare uses the word bitter approximately seventy times in his works. Why does he not use it here? Why does Hamlet not say, "That's bitter." in an aside?

Man has used wormwood for thousands of years. A description of the herb was found on an Egyptian papyrus dated 1600 BC (Kowalchik 509). Wormwood is spoken of in the Geneva Bible of 1560: "And the name of the star is called Wormwood; and the third part of the water became wormwood; and many men died of the waters because they were made bitter" (Revelations 8:11). Wormwood is not spoken of as a poison in the herbals of the sixteenth and seventeenth centuries.

However, that a traditional knowledge of the poisonous qualities of the plant existed cannot be entirely discounted. Poisonous properties of certain plants were sometimes left out of herbals for fear that the knowledge would be used to commit murder (Kowalchik 508). Certainly the poison in wormwood exists. According to modern pharmacologists, the herb can be fatal, especially in the form of absinthe, which is made by distilling the leaves and flowering tops of wormwood. Absinthe is from a first century AD Late Latin participle, absinthiatus meaning flavored with wormwood (Partridge 2). "Absinthe was an addicting and deteriorating drink that led to serious mental disturbances, to seizures, and sometimes to death (Kowalchik 509).

Absinthe was judged to be so lethal that today it is illegal in most countries of the world, including the United States and Canada. France, the major producer of absinthe, finally banned its use in 1915 (Kowalchik 509).

It is in Nicholas Culpeper's Complete Herbal (1653) that we find observations on wormwood that seem to associate the herb with Old Hamlet's death. In order to understand Culpeper's dissertation on wormwood, however, we must first explore the practice of astrological botany. The most famous subscriber of this practice was Theophrastus Bombast von Hohenheim (1493-1541), a professor at Basil who Latinized his name to Paracelsus (Arber 248).

Paracelsus subscribed not only to the doctrine of signatures which held that an herb was good for the body part that it resembled, but also to the idea that each plant was ruled by a particular planet, or astrological botany (Arber 256). Paracelsus perpetuated this strange practice of astrological botany and many others accepted it. Culpeper subscribed fully to the notion and wrote at length about it in his herbal, explaining how the concept affected each herb. "Wormwood is an herb of Mars," he says. He goes on to give many of the same applications for the herb that are found in Dioscorides, Lyte, and Gerard (194-98).

Generally, wormwood in various forms was deemed good against such ailments as choleric stomach, jaundice, windiness and bloating of the stomach and of course as its name indicates, parasitic worms in adults and children. However, when Culpeper begins to expound upon Mar's control of the herb, several of his statements are suggestive of Old Hamlet's symptoms before his death. "Astrologers think Mars causes scabs and itch, and the virgins are angry with him because wanton Venus told them that Mars deforms their skins" (197). According to Culpeper, Mars can cause and cure a disease with the same herb (196). Rodale's modern herbal encyclopedia says even though the oil of wormwood is used in some antiseptic lotions, it is especially dangerous and may cause severe inflammation of the skin if used in full strength (510).

At this juncture, it may be prudent to explore another possibility for the "loathsome crust" that covered Old Hamlet's "smooth body." From his description, the first prospect that comes to mind is some kind of venereal disease. According to Culpeper, wormwood "helps the evils Venus and the wanton Boy produce (196). Since Claudius confesses in his prayer that he did kill his brother Hamlet, there is excessive irony in the idea that Claudius could have used as a poison that which King Hamlet was using for a cure.

Another idea that must be explored further is the suggestion that hebona is a corruption of the word ebony. As stated above, no part of the ebony tree has been found to be poisonous. However, that finding does not cover ebony when it is used as the color black. Of course, a color cannot be poisonous but there is a possible connection here with wormwood. Lady Wilkinson, in Weeds and Wildflowers, tells of an ancient belief about the roots of wormwood "being black and somewhat hard, and remaining for a long period undecayed beneath the living plant. They are called 'wormwood coal'" (Oed353). Could some concoction of this ebony root be the poison that was poured into the "porches" of Old Hamlet's ears?

After all is researched and written, we are really no closer to positively identifying the poison that killed Old Hamlet. However, we at least have another option. Because the evidence supporting hemlock, henbane, Ebenaeace, and the Yew tree is so unlikely, I believe that wormwood, or some admixture of wormwood, must be considered as more likely the toxin as any other suggested.

Until the eighteenth century there were few poisons that were not derived from plants. If Shakespeare knew his plants as well as critics say, then he surely must have intended the poison to be a specific one with which his audience would have been familiar. If he meant hemlock, why not specify hemlock, since he had used it specifically in Henry V, Macbeth, and King Lear? If he meant henbane, why not specify henbane since it was spelled h-e-n-b-a-n-e in the herbals of Maplet, Lyte, Gerard, Parkinson, and Culpeper? These herbals, from Maplet's in 1567 through Culpeper's in 1649, clearly cover the entire life of William Shakespeare.

The alternate spellings of ebony in the OED do not prove that hebona or hebenon in Hamlet means the ebony tree; nor is there any proof of Henry Bradley's suggestion about the Yew tree (87). Connections exist, both in literature and lore, which place wormwood, Artemisia absinthium, high on the list of possible answers to the question of what poison killed Hamlet, the King of Denmark.

SECTION THREE

Ophelia's Herbs

A. A Document in Madness

Ophelia, daughter of Polonius, sister of Laertes, and possible lover of Hamlet -- Rebecca West has said that our modern image of this seventeenth-century flower child comes from a pre-Raphaelite painting by Sir John Millais (1829-1896). The painting represents Ophelia floating downstream, face pale, lips parted, and hands limply open above the water. West says that Millais used as a model a tubercular, timid, and virginal friend who posed lying in a bathtub of water kept warm by a lamp sitting underneath (18).

Many other drawings and portrayals of Ophelia in stage presentations support the image projected by Millais' painting, a pale, flower-bedecked, nonsense-babbling lunatic who has lost all control over her present or future. Whether she is mad, or half-mad, the maid Ophelia retains enough sense to choose the appropriate recipient of each of the herbs she carries. Of course, some critics have disputed this idea. Nikolas Delius even concluded, "the flowers existed only in Ophelia's fantasy and there was no real distribution of real flowers to the persons present" (Furness 346).

However, the idea that Ophelia is actually handing out the flowers is generally accepted. Howard Staunton goes one step further. "There is method to Ophelia's distribution. She presents to each the herb popularly appropriate to his age or disposition"(403).

Rosemary.

"There's rosemary, that's for remembrance; / pray you, love, remember" (4.5.175-6). Ophelia offers the first herb, rosemary, to her brother, Laertes. Rosmarinus officinalis is a perennial evergreen herb. Its needle-like leaves range from green to greenish-gray. Flowers are pale blue, about one-half inch long, and grow in clusters along the branches from December to late spring. Rosemary is a native of the Mediterranean but is widely cultivated in gardens all over the world. In the early twentieth century rosemary was used to preserve meats, especially pork. Today it serves mostly a culinary purpose in chicken and pork dishes.

The folklore surrounding rosemary is as extensive as it is varied in subject. Students in ancient Greece wore rosemary garlands around their heads to improve their memories. Myth has it that the flower was originally white but turned to blue when the Virgin Mary flung her cape on a rosemary bush while fleeing from Herod. In the Middle Ages, a popular practice was putting sprigs of rosemary under the pillow to ward off evil spirits. At funerals, mourners dropped rosemary branches into the grave to show that the dead would not be forgotten (Kowalchik 429). Putting rosemary in the hands of the dead was a French custom. Stories were told of coffins being opened years later to reveal the thriving rosemary that had taken root in the corpse and covered the whole body (Coats 300).

Brewer's Phrase & Fable gives a note on the ancient origin of rosemary: "The shrub is said to be useful in love-making. As Venus, the love Goddess, was sprung from the foam of the sea, rosemary, or sea-dew, would have amatory qualities" (967). The sea-dew idea is the origin of the marinus in rosemary's Latin name, Rosmarinus. Samuel Butler commented on this idea in Hudibras, pt. II, Canto I, 1.843: "The sea his mother Venus came on; / And hence some rev'rend men approve / Of rosemary in making love."

John Gerard lists rosemary's Latin name as Rosmarinus coronaria "because women have been accustomed to make crowns and garlands of it" (1292). Culpeper mentions numerous uses for rosemary, the most interesting of which is "the decoction thereof in wine helps the cold distillations of rheums into the eyes, and all other cold diseases, both of the head, and brain, as the giddiness or swimmings therein, drowsiness or dullness of the mind and senses like a stupidness" (155).

The most common association with rosemary is, as Ophelia says, remembrance. Henry Lyte says, "Rosemary comforteth the brain, the memory, and the inward senses, and it restoreth speech. (188-189). However, rosemary is also associated with both weddings and funerals (Thistelton-Dyer, Folklore of Shakespeare 240-241). This is certainly fitting since Ophelia has been robbed of a wedding, has experienced her father's death and will soon be reason for her own funeral. There is a touch of irony in what poor Ophelia says to her brother. It is shortsighted to maintain that Ophelia urges Laertes only to remember their father. She would much more likely be saying, "Remember me, my ruined life, my treatment at your hands, at our father's hands, and at Hamlet's hands."

Pansy.

"And there is pansies, that's / for thoughts" (4.5.176-7). Memory and thought go hand-in-hand. Therefore, pansies, Viola tricolor, are Ophelia's next offering to Laertes. The pansy can be an annual or a perennial depending upon the variety. Its stems are angular and leafy, while its flower stems are bare with a single flower of yellow, white, or violet. Each flower has five unequal petals. The lower and largest one is notched. The wild pansy is native to the British Isles and the rest of Europe and can be found in mountain pastures or on coastal dunes. It is one of the parents of today's cultivated species of pansy. The pansy has many medicinal and cosmetic properties (Bunney 302).

The name pansy comes from the French word pensee, meaning "thought." It was once the symbol of fidelity (Tergit 192). Many critics believe that the love potion made by Oberon in MND is made from pansies (Coats 219). A most interesting comment comes from John Gerard. He prescribes the pansy as a remedy for French disease, a Renaissance term for venereal disease (852). Skinner gives assorted colloquial names for the pansy, many of them having to do with kissing or fondling (210). However, Shakespeare undoubtedly intended that the pansy indicate just what Ophelia says, "thought." As with remembrance, thought of what is not explained. Possibly again, remember me, think of my ruined life. No father, no lover, no brother.

Harold Jenkins explores a very important point about Shakespeare's intention with the rosemary and pansies: "With rosemary and pansies, the first two flowers, Ophelia indicates and Laertes accepts an emblematic meaning, thereby inviting us to do the same for those [flowers] which follow." Jenkins goes on to say that Shakespeare's audience belonged to an age "more accustomed than our own to emblematic usages" (537). Thus we may expect emblematic meaning to Ophelia's second set of offerings, fennel and rue.

There have been some differences of opinions from critics concerning which herb Ophelia gives to which Royal Highness. Jenkins believes that Ophelia gave fennel and columbines to Gertrude and rue to Claudius. Jenkins' idea on rue is, however, connected to the phrase "with a difference." He considers it a metaphor based on the custom of heraldry in which the younger brothers of a family bear the same arms but with a difference, or with a mark of distinction (348).

I find this suggestion alone enough to discount the theory. Why, at such a poignant moment, would Shakespeare interject a statement on heraldry? Most modern editions of Shakespeare's works, including The Riverside Shakespeare, contain directions that show Ophelia giving fennel and columbines to Claudius and rue and daisies to Gertrude.

Fennel.

"There's fennel for you and columbines" (4.5.180-1). Foeniculum vulgare is a short-lived perennial herb with an erect, bluish-green stem. Its leaves are feathered but fleshy where they attach to the stem. The flowers are yellow and similar in shape to Queen Anne's Lace. All parts of the plant have a licorice or aniseed flavor and fragrance. Fennel is native to the Mediterranean but can be found growing wild in most parts of Great Britain. Fennel has many medicinal properties and is widely used in the food industry today.

The Greek Battle of Marathon, 490 BC, took its name from fennel which is as synonym for marathon in Greek. A youth named Pheidippides ran to Sparta seeking aid for Athens, which was under attack by the Persians. Pan appeared to the youth and promised him victory, giving him a piece of fennel as a token of his prophecy. The battle took place in a field of fennel and was known henceforth as the Battle of Marathon. Statues of the youth, Pheidippides, usually have him holding a branch of fennel.

Robert Browning tells the story very well in his "Pheidippides (Singleton 234). Dioscorides gives numerous medicinal uses for fennel, from drawing down the milk in new mothers to healing dog bites (314). Gerard found fennel too common to describe and gives only one medicinal use, a cure for bad eyesight (242). Culpeper says the herb needs no description and repeats many of Dioscorides' remedies, one of which is to break up kidney stones (73).

Ophelia gives fennel to Claudius. Beisley believes that the gift was meant to suggest that the king needed to clear his sight (158). Without explaining his reason, Bloom says that Ophelia intends to flatter Claudius (85). He may have reached this conclusion because of the many references in literature to fennel as a symbol of flattery. Jenkins cites Green's A Quip for an Upstart Courtier (1592), Jonson's The Case is Altered (1616), and Turbervile's "A Nosegay" (1570), as referring to fennel as symbolic of flattery (537-39).

However, considering the satyr-like image of Claudius in the play, it seems just as likely that Shakespeare intended another, or an additional meaning for the gift of fennel. Alice Coats mentions a tradition that "sowing fennel is sowing sorrow, but if you give it away disaster will follow" (285).

Certainly the recipients of Ophelia's offerings met with disaster. Henry Lyte gives several medicinal recipes for fennel, most of which are concerned with the kidneys and other internal organs. One recipe is to help fill "women's breasts or dugs with milk." Lyte adds, "Fennel berries in Wine is very good for the secret part of man, to be either bathed or rubbed and anointed with the same" (193). Staunton maintains that the fennel presented to the King suggested flattery but also lust (403). F.G. Savage sees no room for argument: "Fennel here means lustful cajolery" (269). Thistelton-Dyer explains: "Fennel is hot and dry in the third degree and was generally considered inflammatory" (Folklore of Shakespeare 217).

In 2H4, when Falstaff says that Poins "eats conger [a species of eel] and fennel," he means that Poins eats two very hot things together (2.4). Since both flattery and lust seem to have been relatively well known in association with fennel, it is not too far-fetched to assume that Shakespeare made full use of the connotations of both.

Columbine.

"There's fennel for you, and columbines" (4.5.180-1). Aquilegia vulgaris, columbine, is common in the wild in Europe, the British Isles, and America. This rather unusual herb is easily distinguished because of its foliage, which resembles the shamrock and its bloom which hangs at the top of a bare stem. It has been likened to several birds clinging together with their wings expanded. The columbine grows easily from seed but different colors will not stay true when grown in the same garden.

There are conflicting opinions in the old herbals about columbine and its medicinal value and whether or not it was known by the ancients. Henry Lyte says that it did not grow in England and was "unknown of the ancients." Also, "some of the new writers do affirm it to be good against the jaundice (119).

Gerard says that columbine was used in making garlands and that the seeds, boiled in water, are good to hasten women's labors (447). Culpeper says that columbine was so common in England that he doesn't find it necessary to give a description of it. He calls it "Herb of Venus" which suggests it has sexually related properties (53).

Gervase Markham lists a recipe that he cites as composed by Hippocrates (certainly an ancient) and which contains columbine and other herbs with limail (metal filings) and other ingredients such as the urine of a male child, woman's milk, and egg whites. This extraordinary concoction was good for severe headaches and to make a man "look young even in old age"(129). Tergit says that the columbine was one of the most common flowers that Renaissance women used to make perfume (212).

Both Beisley (158) and Grindon (172) quote from George Chapman's Comedy of All Fools (1605): "What's that? A columbine / No! that thankless flower grows not in my garden." Neither Beisley nor Grindon can explain the origin of "thankless." However, Beisley uses the idea to support his assertion that Ophelia offers the king the columbine "as both she and her brother Laertes believed that the King had killed Polonius, their father" (158). Staunton calls columbine symbolic of "ingratitude" but fails to explain that origin (403). Savage quotes from William Brown's Britannia's Pastorals (1613): "The columbine by lonely wand'rer taken, Is there ascribed to such as are forsaken" (161).

Thistelton-Dyer says, "The columbine was once known as Herba lionis, from a belief that it was a lion's favorite plant" (Folklore 263). The lion is commonly known as king. The OED's description of columbine makes the herb a most appropriate gift for Claudius. "The horned nectaries suggested to an earlier age allusions to cuckoldry" (642).

Thus, Ophelia's offerings of fennel and columbine to Claudius the King who has, at least inadvertently, robbed her of all who were dear to her, are symbols of ingratitude, lust, and cuckoldry.

Rue.

"There's rue for you, and some for me; we may call it herb of grace a'Sundays. You may wear rue with a difference (4.5.181-3). Ruta graveolens is a perennial evergreen shrub. Its stems are woody at the base but are green and tender at the top. Rue emits a pungent odor that some people find offensive. Its blooms are yellow and appear in lacy clusters at the top of the plant. Rue is a native of Southern Europe and Northern Africa. The genus name Ruta comes from the Greek reuo and means "to set free." Ruth was the Old English word for pity and compassion. Thus rue became associated with Ruth thereby gaining its virtues of sorrow and repentance. Even today, we may hear it used thusly, "You'll rue this day forever!"

Pliny mentions rue briefly as good to make a draught that will make a man "beareth his drink well, and withstand the fumes that might trouble and intoxicate his brains"(Holland 182). Dioscorides lists dozens of uses for rue, including as a mouthwash, an antidote to poison, and as an abortive agent (286).

Lyte gives twenty medicinal uses for rue, most of which are listed in Dioscorides and Pliny's herbals. One of them, however, seems specifically related to Ophelia's state of mind: "the juice of rue with vinegar given to smell unto, both revive and quicken such as have the lethargie" (187). Bankes Herbal gives instructions for a combination eyewash. "Also, an ointment for sore-eyes: stamp fennel and rue together, and meddle them with honey and euphrasy, and it is good ointment for the eyes" (71).   Maybe Claudius and Gertrude needed their visions cleared?

Until the nineteenth century, rue was used to strew the floors of English law courts as a guard against the spread of diseases. Because of its strangely shaped leaves, rue served as the model for the playing card club (Tergit 38).

Ophelia obviously regards rue basically as an emblem of grief for both herself and the queen. Furness contends that when she says, "we may call it herb of grace o' Sundays," she means that Queen Gertrude may "with peculiar propriety on Sundays, when she solicits pardon, call her 'rue' 'herb of grace' " (348).

"You may wear your rue with a difference" means that rue for the queen "should be the emblem of something more than simple grief--contrition with regard to the past" (Grindon 204). This seems a sound assertion. Ophelia's reason to wear rue is in grief for her father's death, and her loss of lover and brother. She is innocent of blame in these losses. Queen Gertrude, however, is guilty of participating in an incestuous marriage and of being at least an accessory after the fact of her husband's murder. She may therefore wear her rue out of guilt and grief.

Notes and Queries, March 10, 1883, quotes George Wither (1588-1667) and the fifth editor of Shakespeare, William Warburton (1698-1779) on other possible clues to this topic. "Rue was a principal ingredient in the potion which the Romish priests used to forced the 'possessed' to swallow down when they exorcised them. The fact that these exorcisms were performed generally on a Sunday, in the church before the whole congregation, is the reason Ophelia says, 'We may call it 'Herb of grace o' Sundays' " (193). Lines from Wither's Britains Remembrancer express the same sentiments: "He must avoid the crimes he lived in: / His Physicke must be Rue (ev'n Rue for sinne) / Of Herb of Grace a cordiall he must make; / The bitter cup of true Repentance take" (193). Another suggestion comes from Bunney: "Brushes made from the plant were used in churches to sprinkle holy water on Sundays before High Mass and this supposedly is the reason for the old name Herb of Grace or Herbygrass" (254).

There are several other interesting notes about rue that seem fitting when associated with Gertrude. "Rue is said to be conducive to chastity" (Tergit 231). From William Coles' Schola Salerne: "Rue maketh chaste and eke [also] preserveth sight" (Savage 7:260). Skinner says, "It keeps maids from going wrong in affairs of love, if only they will pause to eat or wear it when tempted" (261). All of this is sound advice, but imparted too late to save Old Hamlet and the Kingdom of Denmark.

Daisy.

"There's a daisy" (4.5.184). The daisy offered to Gertrude by Ophelia was probably the Bellis perennis, a common, short-stemmed little flower that can still be seen in great numbers in the lawns of Stratford, England. This daisy has a solitary flower head with a yellow center surrounded by white petals that may turn pale pink as it ages.

Thiselton-Dyer speaks of the custom that dates back to the Middle Ages of lovers testing the sincerity of their partner's affections by plucking off the daisy petals one by one, chanting, "He/she loves me, He/she loves me not (94). Thiselton-Dyer also addresses the suggestion that one common name for the English daisy, "herb-Margaret," came from the association with the virtuous St. Margaret of Antioch.

He also cites an old legend that tells of a daisy-like flower that is called herb-Margaret and which is traditionally scattered at the shrine of St. Margaret of Cortona. "Apparently, this saint had many sins to do penance for" (228).

Lyte gives several medicinal uses for the daisy, most of them good for diseases of internal organs (121). Gerard offers several recipes for medicine, the most unusual being: "The juice of the leaves and roots given to the little dogs in milk keepeth them from growing great" (203). Culpeper says the daisy is so well known it needs no description, that it is good for breast wounds and that it is under the dominion of Venus (61). Also, the daisy is good "against the King's evil [scrofula]" (le Strange 53).

Greene, in A Quip for an Upstart Courtier explains about the daisy: "Next them grew the dissembling daisie, to warn of such light-of-love wenches not to trust every faire promise that such amorous bachelors make them" (Furness 348).

The daisy has the least obvious symbolic significance of all the flowers that Ophelia offers. However, use of the daisy seems too germane to ignore. Chaucer, in "The Legend of Good Women," mentions Alceste "That turned was into a dayesye [daisy] / She that for hire housbonde chees to dye" (602). Gertrude dies, in a sense, for her husband, Old Hamlet, who is at the root of all that happens in the play.

Could this offering of a daisy be another of Ophelia's subtle prophecies of disaster such as she seemed to make with the fennel?

Violet.

"I would give you some violets, but / they wither'd all when my father died" (4.5.184-5). Viola odorata is a perennial herb with a rhizome root. Leaves are rounded and toothed and grow in a rosette from which rises single stems with single, fragrant, drooping blossoms. The blossom has five petals, two upper that are erect, two center ones that spread out to the side, and one lower petal that curls slightly toward the stem. The center of the blossom is orange surrounded by a thin border of white. Viola odorata grows throughout Europe and in some countries it is cultivated commercially for the perfume industry.

Skinner gives an excellent account of the early lore surrounding the violet: The violet sprang from Io, a priestess in Juno's temple with whom Jupiter was almost caught in one of his flirtations. Not having time to conceal her, he changed her into a white heifer; but grass not being good enough for so delicate a creature, the God created the violet as her special food.

Greeks consecrated the violet to Jupiter, Athenians made it their symbol of their city. When a Greek was buried, his body was concealed with violets so the grave was carpeted with color and fragrance. After the Old Gods died, the lore of the violet was transferred to the Virgin. The story is that the shadow of the cross fell on it and it drooped its head in sorrow. Is color is the purple of church mourning (105).

Savage gives a piece of lore that predates the Virgin story. The tears of repentance that Adam shed when God forgave him dropped on the ground and violets grew (29). Tergit gives the violet as the symbol of innocence throughout Europe over the centuries (28).

Lyte offers a list of remedies made from violets, many of which can be found in modern books on herbal medicines. Violets are good against fevers, inflammation, coughs, ague, sore throat, falling sickness, headache, insomnia, and constipation. In addition Lyte says, "It is of a very pleasant and amiable smell" (105).

Lyte (105), Gerard (198), and Culpeper (189), say that the violet is "under the sign of Venus," which signifies its association with lust. Culpeper says it makes a cure for the "French pox" [syphilis] (190).

Beisley states simply, "It was well known for its fragrance" (421). Ellacombe is careful to point out, "In all passages where Shakespeare names the violet, he alludes to the purple sweet-scented violet (246). Singleton quotes Bacon who thought the violet to be, "that which above all others yields the sweetest smell (125). Bloom says that the most constant theme in violets in Shakespeare is their fragrance (152).

Certainly Shakespeare uses the idea of fragrance in his first reference to violets in Hamlet. Laertes compares Hamlet to a violet, suggesting that Hamlet's attentions are as short-lived as the fragrance of that flower which blooms in the spring for only a short while.

Ophelia's statement that all the violets had withered when her father died is more difficult to associate with scent. Jenkins connects it with the withering of Hamlet's love for Ophelia, and he also suggests that Ophelia has confused Polonius with Hamlet in her grief over her losses (541). It seems more likely that Ophelia is remembering Polonius' service to Denmark (1.2.47-9), and is thinking of the Greek practice of carpeting the body in its grave with violets for both the display of color and the purifying fragrance (Skinner 105).

The last time that Shakespeare mentions violets in Hamlet obviously alludes to fragrance. Laertes calls for violets to spring from Ophelia's "fair and unpolluted flesh." Charlotte Otten believes that when Laertes prays for violets, he recognizes that they are appropriate burial plants that are meant to offset the foul odor of the grave (118).

Laertes calls his sister "a document in madness." However, whether she is mad or not, Ophelia's offerings carried with them information that must have been important to Shakespeare's audience in their understanding the major characters in Hamlet.

B. The Satirical Diadem

In The World of Shakespeare, Alan Dent comments briefly on Ophelia's fantastic garland and says, "Most of the scholars and editors completely ignore three lines in Hamlet, (4.7.168-70) in the course of Gertrude's description of the manner in which the sad Ophelia drowned herself" (Dent 316). I heartily agree but I would add lines 166-67 and line 171. The "fantastic garland" is most fascinating and is made even more so when introduced by the willow.

Willow.

"There's a willow grows askaunt the brook / That shows his hoary leaves in the glassy stream" (4.7.166-7). Salix alba is a deciduous medium-sized tree with grayish bark, yellowish stems and long, slim leaves that are alternately serrated. The leaves' undersides are grayish-white (hoary). Stalkless male and female blossoms appear directly from woody stems. Salix alba is native to Britain and flourishes in wet or moist areas (Bunney 255).

It is not the cultivated weeping-willow tree seen in landscape plantings but the white willow that is commonly found growing on creek banks. The white willow leaves are silvery underneath and would certainly reflect in the water.

Skinner gives the ancient lore of the willow. (1) The sisters of Phaeton were turned to willow as they mourned his death. Cascades of their tears turned to flowing willow branches; thus the willow tree loves dampness. (2) One variety of the willow has been planted in cemeteries in China for thousands of years. (3) The willow preserved Orpheus when he descended into hell. (4) The tree bears a curse because Judas hanged himself on one. (5) The devil planted a willow to lure people by the restful swaying of its branches to commit suicide. (6) One variety of willow was used to make beds for maidens in the festival of Ceres, where they could sleep and retain their innocence. (7) In the Middle Ages, monks made belts of willow because they believed that it withstood uncleanness and quenched desires of the flesh (296-97).

Both old and modern herbals support the ancient lore of the willow. According to Dioscorides, "Being taken of themselves [the leaves] with water, they cause inconception" (75).

Lyte says that, among other uses, "The greene leaves found very small, and laid about the private member, do take away the desire to lechery" (535). Culpeper stresses the same idea. "The leaves bruised and boiled in wine, and drank, stays the head of lust in man or woman, and quite extinguishes it, if it be long used" (192). Maude Grieve lists Salix alba as an aphrodisiac and as a cure for gonorrhea.

Also, it was used to relieve ovarian pain and in the treatment of nocturnal emissions (847).

According to Bloom, the sixteenth century poets looked upon the willow solely as a symbol of jilted love (149). Ellacombe discusses the many practical uses such as material for weaving baskets and building willow huts, and in the "wattle 'n' daub" construction of fences and walls. However, Ellacombe does say, "The sole use of willow for the poets was to weave garlands for jilted lovers, male and female" (254).

Shakespeare uses the willow in both of these senses. "Make me a willow cabin at your gate" (TN 1.5.269). "I wear the willow garland for his sake" (3H6 3.3.228). Yet the most poignant instance is when Gertrude begins to tell Laertes of Ophelia's death. "There's a willow grows askaunt the brook, / That shows his hoary leaves in the glassy stream" (Hamlet 5.1.166-67).

This seems an appropriate place to clear up one misconception about what took place with Ophelia at the stream. Ophelia was not wearing the garland when she fell into the water. She was "clamb'ring to hang" them on a branch just as the Biblical fathers did in Psalms 137.2: "We hanged our harps upon the willow in the midst thereof."

The limb broke; she lost her balance, and fell into the water. This belies the image put forth by most illustrations of Ophelia floating wistfully in the water with her "crownet weeds" in place around her head.

Crow-flower.

"Therewith fantastic garlands did she make / Of crow-flowers, nettles, daisies, and long purples, / That liberal shepherds give a grosser name" (4.7.168-70). There is a strong difference of opinion among critics on what plant the crow-flower is meant to be. Ellacombe (51), Thiselton-Dyer (Folklore 212), Savage (17), and Jenkins (545), all suggest the Ragged Robin or Lychnis flos-cuculi. Their opinion is based mainly on a statement from Gerard. "They (Ragged Robin) serve for garlands and crowns (62).

Both Grindon and Singleton say the crow-flower is the hyacinth, Scilla rutans. According to Singleton, the hyacinth is a symbol of pure and faithful love (207). Grindon argues that the Ragged Robin could not possibly be the right herb because it does not bloom at the same time as the other plants in the garland (127-28).

Beisley (159) and Bloom (34) say the common yellow buttercup, Ranunculus replans, is the plant Ophelia used mainly because it blooms at the appropriate time. The buttercup would also be appropriate in form and color for a garland but it has a terrible odor.

Bloom believes the buttercup is appropriate because it stinks and is also poisonous. He suggests that these attributes make the plant fitting for the garland because all the other plants in the garland are "baneful in their attributes" (34). Also, many ranunculus varieties were commonly called crowfoot in England (OED 1208).

Dioscorides says the Ranunculus grows near running water and he gives several common medicinal uses for it

(217). Culpeper writes, "Virgins, in ancient times, used to make a powder of them to furrow brides beds" (59).[2]

Grieve gives many medicinal uses for Ranunculus but also stresses the danger of blistering the skin when handling the plant (235-36). Tergit says the buttercup was used in ancient Egypt to make floral crowns (18).

As with other herbs in Shakespeare, there is no way to prove the absolute identity of the crow-flower. However, the Ranunculus, or common buttercup, seems fitting in more ways that the Ragged Robin or the hyacinth for these reasons: (1) The buttercup blooms at the right time; (2) The buttercup was also called crowfoot or crow-flower; (2) The bloom size and bright color would work well in a garland; (4) The buttercup grows in damp places or near running water; (5) The buttercup has some history of being used to make floral crowns. In addition, as Bloom believes, the fact that it stinks and is poisonous makes it appropriate for a garland of "baneful attributes" (34).

Nettle.

As with most of the other herbs associated with Ophelia, there is considerable difference of opinion about which variety of nettle she uses in her garland. Beisley (159), Bloom (33-34), and Savage (53) prefer Lamium

---

[2]   The OED gives "to wrinkle or gather up in folds" as a definition of "furrow" and I have been unable to find any other reference to this statement.

album, commonly called Dead Nettle or White Nettle. Lamium album has no stingers and it flowers in May. Ellacombe believes Urtica diocia to be nettle that Shakespeare uses in his works at least a dozen times (135). This variety is edible, but is also covered with stingers and its bloom is scant and not of a shape or color to make it desirable or suitable for weaving into a garland.

Grindon (128) and Grieve (579) think the appropriate nettle to be Galeobdolon luteum. This variety has a beautiful yellow bloom, no stingers, and it would be blooming at the appropriate time. However, this nettle has a very disagreeable odor (Grieve 580).

Lyte says that nettles are all very much alike in their remedial virtues. "The same drunken with sweete wine dothe stirre up bodily pleasure" (129). Gerard agrees. "The seed of the nettle stirreth up lust especially when drunk with Cute [OED, a boiled wine]." Culpeper gives many uses for the nettle but comments that "others think it only powerful to provoke venery (127).

There is no definite answer to which nettle Ophelia used in her fantastic garland. Both the Lamium album and the Galeobdolon luteum are possibilities. However, based on Charlotte Otten's theory called the "ontology of smells," which I will talk about later, my choice is Galeobdolon luteum because of the disagreeable odor that Grieve mentions (580).

Daisy.

Bellis perennis we have already covered in chapter 2. However, additional information comes from Alice Coats and may be seen as appropriate to a girl about to meet her death, as Ophelia certainly is. "This innocent flower derives its Latin name from the word meaning 'war' because of its supposed value on the battlefield in staunching the wounds of the fallen; and 'to lie beneath the daisies' [or a more modern, more flippant term, pushing up daisies] has become a synonym for death" (32).

Long Purples.

This plant has given botanists and literary critics who have condescended to notice it the most reason for conjecture of any plant mentioned in the Shakespeare canon. Nevertheless, seldom does a critic explain beyond stating that there is some phallic symbolism associated with the plant and that the name given it by "liberal shepherds" is both vulgar and crude.

The two plants most commonly thought to be long purples are Orchis mascula and Arum maculatum. The main problem in correctly identifying the appropriate herb is that each of these fits the part extremely well.

Orchis mascula is a perennial herb with roots of ovoid shaped tubers. Its leaves are lanceolate, broad in the center, and spotted. The bottom leaves form a rosette; the upper ones sheath the flower stem. The blossoms are purple-red and slightly resemble the modern snapdragon (Martin).

The Orchis, according to Skinner, was born, as were so many of our plants, in ancient Greece. Orchis was the son of a nymph and a satyr and as a result he was a "fellow of unbounded passion." At a Bacchus festival, Orchis was drunk and attacked a priestess. The enraged congregation tore him limb from limb. Orchis' father, the satyr, begged the gods to reassemble Orchis' parts and make him whole again but they refused.

However, out of pity for the father, they agreed to change him into a flower. "Even the flower was alleged to retain his temper, and to eat its root was to summer momentary conversion into the satyr state" (205-6).

The earliest herbals that we have access to in modern times continue this association of the Orchis with lust and lechery. Dioscorides lists four kinds of Orchis: Orchis rubra, Orchis eteros, Saturion eruthronion, and Saturion, all very much alike. Orchis means "testicle" in Greek (OED), and the word is used specifically in Dioscorides' description of the tubers. "The root lies under like the Testicle. If the greater root is eaten by man, he will beget male children, from the lesser come female children" (373-74).

Women in Thessalia gave the tender root, ground up and mixed with goat's milk, to provoke lust, and the other dry one to discourage lust. One of the varieties "ought to be drunk in black hard wine" before lying with a woman. One of them "being taken into the hand doth provoke to Venerie, but much more, being drunk with wine" (Dioscorides 373-74).

Pliny describes the Orchis frankly: "The root likewise is bulbous and two-fold, fashioned like a man's stones or cullions; of which the bigger, (as some say) the harder, drunk in water, provoketh the desire to venery: the lesser and softer taken in goat's milk represseth the aforesaid appetite" (Holland 246).

Maplet says the Orchis "helps in digestion and satisfieth Nature's desires" (109). Lyte describes five varieties of Orchis, all of which are similar. He repeats the virtues and uses given by Dioscorides and Pliny, and gives a long list of common names, most blatantly phallic: Dog's

Cods, Priests pintle [penis], Ballock [testicle] grass, Fooles Balloxe, Goats Cullions, Serapias stones, and flie Orchis (156-59).

Gerard gives the Orchis the same virtues for arousing lust and also offers a list of common names, a few of which are Fox Stones, Finger Orchis, Soldiers Cullions, Marish Satyrion, Soldiers Satyrion, Gelded Satyrion, and Serapias Stones (205-8). Of the Serapias stones Gerard says their blossoms are like "flies and such like fruitful and lascivious insects, as taking their name from Serapias the god of the citizens of Alexandria in Egypt, who had a most famous Temple at Canopus, where he was worshipped with all kinds of lascivious wantonness, songs, and dances, as we may read in Strabo, in his seventeenth booke" (225). Gerard also says the Orchis has a "rank and stinking smell" (209).

Culpeper describes the Orchis in lengthy detail and then lists its qualities: "They are hot and moist in operation and under the dominion of Dame Venus, and provoke lust exceedingly, which, they say, the dried and withered roots restrain. Being bruised and applied to the place, they do cure the King's evil" (130).

Grieve says that witches used the tubers of Orchis mascula in their love potions. The fresh roots were to provoke lust, the dried ones to check wrong passion (603).

Beisley believes the Orchis mascula to be the long purples in Hamlet. He bases his argument on the shape of the tubers, saying, "This unequal size of the bulbs might probably have given rise to one of the vulgar names used by the liberal shepherds in sixteenth century" (160-61).

However, Shakespeare, in his "manly delicacy" withholds the vulgar name from the lips of the queen. The clue lies, Grindon says, in "dead men's fingers," a name given originally to the Orchis masculata and passed on to the Orchis mascula because of the similarities of the tubers. It is quite obvious that Grindon bases his opinion on the "strange similitude of the tubers to the male genitalia (129).

Ellacombe suggests the long purples could be any one of three orchis varieties: morio, masculata, or mascula. Some have palmate roots, which could have inspired "dead men's fingers." He admits rather reluctantly that the "grosser" names can be found in the old Herbals (114).

Savage mentions the Orchis as a possibility and says, "Were it permissible to publish an extremely local name it would be possible to throw a good deal of light on the grosser name of the liberal shepherds in favour of this flower" (48). Jenkins gives the Orchis mascula as the favored flower (545). George Stevens (1736-1800) called the various names of the long purples "too gross for repetition" but says they can be found in Lyte's Herbal (Furness 371n.). Furness also quotes Edmond Malone (1741-1812): "One of the grosser names Gertrude had a particular reason to avoid, the rampant widow" (371n.).

While it seems that the case for long purples as Orchis mascula is extremely difficult to refute, there is just as much pertinent and persuasive information on the Arum maculatum, a perennial herb with a single tuber from which grow many fine roots. A thick stem grows directly from the tuber and is surrounded by long-stemmed sagittae leaves.

The single flower stem bears a "pale yellow-green trumpet shaped spathe, edged and sometimes spotted with purple, which encloses a purplish, cylindrical flowerhead called a spadix" (Bunney 78). For most American readers, the best description of the Arum would be a variety of Jack-in-the-Pulpit, Arum triphyllum, which grows in woodlands in nearly all areas of eastern North America.

Again, Skinner provides the ancient lore of the herb in question. Israel's spies carried Aaron's rod when they went into the Promised Land. Across the rod they carried great bunches of grapes and other fruits. Upon arrival in the Promised Land, they stuck the rod in the ground and the Arum grew as a symbol of abundance and fertility (52).

Dioscorides likens the Arum bloom to a serpent and says the plant is "destructive of Embrya newly conceived" (207). Maplet calls the Arum "Wake Robin" and says it "satisfies natures desires, being once taken" (109).

William Coles, who carried the doctrine of signatures to the extreme (Arber 252), says of Arum: "It hath not only the signature which will sufficiently declare itself but the virtue also according to the signature, for they [the Arum] are notable for stirring up of inclination to copulation, being either well-roasted under the embers, or boiled" (38).

Lyte's description of Arum explains its common names. "It has…from which riseth a stalk of a span long, spotted here and there with some purple specks, and it carieth a certain long codde, huske, or hose, open by one side." Some of the common names are Aron, Priests pintle, Cuckow-pintle, and Wake-Robin (371-72).

Gerard lists the names of Arum as Cuckow pintle, Wake-Robin, Priests pintle, Aron, Calfes foot, and Starchwort. He tells a strange story about bears coming out of their dens after forty days and searching for the Arum, which they eat to open their "hungry gut" which has shrunk from abstaining from food. He mentions the starch made from the powdered root, which was used to stiffen the Elizabethan neck-ruffle (304).

Culpeper lists Arum under the name Cuckow-pint and not surprisingly says it is under the dominion of Mars. He gives many medicinal uses for the herb but steers rather coyly away from direct mention of lust or lechery. "Authors have left large commendation of this herb, you see, but for my part, I have neither spoken with Dr. Reason nor Dr. Experience about it" (60-61).

Bloom believes that Arum is the long purple of Ophelia's garland. He doubts that anyone in Shakespeare's age would have noticed the flower or root of the Orchis.[3] He suggests the Arum because its spadix bears a resemblance to a dead man's finger wrapped in a green winding sheet. However, he mentions that the grosser name, cuckoopint, is ready at hand (33-34).

Maude Grieve's description of the arum is very suggestive of its common names. "The flowering organs are contained in a sheath-like leaf." Like Gerard, Grieve mentions that arum roots were ground and cooked into

---

[3]   I believe the emphasis in the most popular herbals of the day is sufficient to refute this doubt.

starch to stiffen the Elizabethan neck-ruffle (236-37). Surely this means the plant was relatively well known?

Joseph Krutch believes the long purple to be Arum. He says folk imagination gave many appropriate common names to herbs based on the doctrine of signatures and that "No signature is more modestly evident than that provided by the very phallic central column [of the Arum]." Krutch connects the common name Wake-Robin to Ophelia's song. "Wake-Robin (though now gently poetic) was clear enough to those same Elizabethans who snickered when the mad Ophelia sang, 'For bonnie sweet Robin is all my joy'" (4.5.187).

Henry Morris comments on the name Robin that was "in the sixteenth century, one of the cant [common] terms for the male sex organ" (602). Alan Dent guesses that the long purple is the Arum because of the "stout spike projecting upwards" (361).

Karl Wentersdorf, in Shakespeare Quarterly 29 (1978), argues against the Orchis Mascula and for the Arum maculatum as the long purples. He suggests the Arum because it seems more appropriate for dead men's fingers and "Partly because the Arum's phallic spadix is surrounded by a partially opened whitish sheath that could be thought of as a shroud, and partly because the term 'finger' can be a euphemism for the phallus" (416).

One year later, Charlotte Otten, in Shakespeare Quarterly 30 (1979), took Wentersdorf to task for his statement that proponents of the Orchis base their arguments on "an improbable concatenation of guesses" (Wentersdorf

417). Otten bases her argument for the Orchis on the "extensive catalog of grosser names and the lewd botanical-medical history of Orchids: for centuries they appeared in copulatory texts" (397).

Otten condenses her argument into five points, four of which are appropriate both for their comment on the Orchis and for the herb's relationship to Ophelia's situation: "(1) that the Greek and Latin names for Orchis and testiculus were adopted because the roots resemble testicles and arouse carnal desires; (2) that the 'grosser names'...connoted the organs of generation to Gertrude and her audience; (3) that the name Satyrion, an ancient allusion to the satyr...is particularly appropriate in the incestuous kingdom where Hamlet refers to Claudius as a satyr (1.2.140); (4) that Serapias stones was an indication of rank and gross adultery, the kind Hamlet ascribes to Claudius and Gertrude: 'Stewe'd in corruption, honeying and making love / Over the nasty sty!' (3.4.93-94)." ("Ophelia's Long Purples'" 401-402).

I must admit that Otten makes a good case for the Orchis as the long purple of Ophelia's "fantastic Garland." However, the overall implications are the same as they are for the Arum.

Therefore, with either herb, we are left with a harmless but mad young girl burdened with a wreath of herbs, all of which are, in varying degrees, clearly associated with gross sexual lust and lechery.

Primrose.

"But, good my brother, / Do not, as some ungracious pastors do, / Show me the steep and thorny way to heaven, / Whiles, [like] a puff'd and reckless libertine, / Himself the primrose path of dalliance treads" (1.3.49-50). This herb Primrose must be explored because of its symbolic importance to the entire play.

Primula vulgaris grows profusely throughout Great Britain. A perennial herb, its roots are thick and fibrous and sprout from a short, stocky single rhizome. The leaves of the Primrose are ovate to oblong, serrated, slightly furry, and arranged in a rosette that grows directly from the rhizome. Bloom stems grow from the center of the rosette and bear clusters of deep yellow flowers that are sweet-scented. The places most conducive to abundant growth of the Primrose are woods and shady banks or hedgerows.

Primula vulgaris has for centuries been associated with places where sinful pleasures may be indulged in, i.e., the "primrose path." Brathwait (1611) used the idea in Golden Fleece: "For she [Rosamond] did flourish for a while / Cropt in the primrose of her wantonesse" (2. Sonnet 4.3) (OED). Shakespeare uses the association in A Midsummer Night's Dream when lovesick Hermia says to Lysander, "And in the wood where you and I / upon faint primrose-beds were wont to lie" (1.1.215).

A much stronger statement is made in Macbeth when the porter at the symbolical gates of hell says, "I had thought to have let in some of all professions that go the primrose path to th' everlasting bonfire" (2.3.1-21). In Hamlet,

Ophelia admonishes her brother and suggests he not be like hypocritical pastors who may preach chastity "While, a puff'd and reckless libertine / Himself the primrose path of dalliance treads" (1.3.50).

Although the Primrose is considered an herb and was in use before, during, and after the Renaissance for many medicinal purposes, none of its Renaissance uses is even remotely suggestive of sexual pleasures. Apparently, it is where the herb grows and flourishes, in woods and shady places, which gave birth to its connection with sexual pleasure.

The OED gives "path of pleasure" as one definition of the Primrose. Another is "a pretty young woman" (168). In "The Miller's Tale," Chaucer says of his lascivious Alison, "She was a prymerole [M.E. primrose], a piggesnye (3268). Here Chaucer connects the primrose to an herb that has been discussed earlier. The OED gives "piggesnye" as one of the names applied to Ragged Robin and the Cuckoo flower, both of which are common names for Ophelia's crude "long purples."

The idea of treading the primrose path for sexual pleasure survives in the twentieth century. It can be heard frequently in casual speech. In the 1960's a popular rock group recorded a song that rose to the top of the charts. The title was "Primrose Lane." The singer begs his sweetheart to join him because, "life's a holiday on primrose lane with me."

Nigel Alexander says, "The 'primrose path' is the road to hell and the entire family [in Hamlet} is in danger of taking it. Polonius follows it as a servant of a king whose whole power is based upon such sexual dalliance. Laertes follows it when he returns to avenge his father" (134).

It is my conclusion, however, that Ophelia, more than any other character in Hamlet is the person who is led down the "primrose path of dalliance." She was literally led by her father, and cruelly and emotionally led by Hamlet.

C. *Ophelia*

The purpose of the character of Ophelia in Hamlet is not easy to define. The most common opinion of Ophelia's function lies somewhere between "a character almost too exquisitely touching to be dwelt upon" as William Hazlitt saw her (111), and "Shakespeare's pathetic plot device" as Wagner sees her (94).

Certainly we cannot deny Ophelia as Hazlitt describes her, "a flower too soon faded" (111). However, under close examination the Ophelia character emerges much nearer to Wagner's interpretation. Wagner says that Ophelia has two primary purposes: that of providing a convenient hinge for several of Hamlet's analytical scenes" and "that of providing the emotional impact for the audience" (94).

Although closer to actuality than Hazlitt's evaluation, Wagner stops short of a complete definition of Ophelia's purpose. Wagner says Ophelia is "used by Hamlet, Polonius, and Shakespeare himself" (94). However, Ophelia, of a certainty, serves a much broader and more important purpose than that presented by Wagner.

Shakespeare uses Ophelia like a narrator who gives the audience details that add to their understanding of the characters and their situations and actions. This position is only figurative, of course; she does not stand to one side of the stage and read a prepared script. Her role is subtler as she makes her speeches with the aid of various props that suggest one consistent state: sexual corruption.

Rebecca West calls Ophelia "one of the few authentic portraits of that army of not virgin martyrs, the poor little girls who were sacrificed to family ambition in the days when a court was a cat's cradle of conspiracies" (21). It was in this network of conspiracy that Ophelia was used by her father.

In his eagerness to please his king, Polonius offers to find the truth of Hamlet's madness. The old adviser says, "I'll loose my daughter to him" (2.2.162).[1]

Dover Wilson says that Polonius meant that he would make Ophelia sexually available to Hamlet. Wilson cites other passages from Shakespeare's works where the term "loose" is used in the same contest. He says he has also heard the word used by farmers as they discussed the breeding of cattle and horses, and that confirmation of the meaning comes when Polonius speaks a few lines later in the same discussion of a "farm and carter."

---

[1]   [14] OED loose: free from moral restraint, lax in principle, conduct or speech: chiefly in a narrower sense, unchaste, wanton, dissolute, immoral.

Wilson supports his interpretation further by quoting other sexually suggestive words that are spoken in the same passage by Hamlet to Polonius. According to Wilson (and substantiated in the OED),"fishmonger" is another word for "pimp," "carrion" can mean "flesh" in the carnal sense, while "conception" speaks for itself (104-5).

Ironically, earlier in the play both Polonius (1.2.115-35) and Laertes (1.3.10-44) caution Ophelia about Hamlet's attentions toward her. Nigel Alexander says both the father's and the brother's warnings "contain a strong libidinous undercurrent of sexuality. They regard her as a girl of vibrant personality who must restrain and 'understand' herself in order not to ally herself with her lover. Both speeches picture Ophelia as seduced, made pregnant, and abandoned by Hamlet" (136-37).

In the passages just mentioned, about whom do we attain the most information? Most decidedly not Ophelia! We learn that Laertes is a hypocrite, and that Polonius does not hesitate to bargain his daughter's favors when the situation is to his advantage.

Critics generally agree about the strong atmosphere of sexuality in Hamlet. The basis for the idea of sexual corruption seems to stem from Hamlet's perception of his mother as offered to him by the Ghost. Gertrude was "a seeming virtuous queen" who overindulged herself "in a celestial bed" and preyed "on garbage" (1.5. 46, 55-56). The Ghost slyly cautions Hamlet not to allow his mind to be tainted by the image of his mother in her bed, "a couch for luxury and damned incest" (1.5.84).

However, Hamlet's mind is tainted, stained, even infected by the unwholesome, incestuous images projected for him by the Ghost. Hamlet's perception of the image reveals his tainted, infected mind as he later recalls it to his mother: "In the rank sweat of an enseamed bed, / Stew'd in corruption, honeying and making love / Over the nasty sty" (3.4.93-94).

Hamlet obviously transfers to Ophelia his disgust at things sexual. In their first encounter in the play, he asks her, "Are you honest? (3.1.102). Furness quotes Howard Staunton (1810-1874): "that 'honest' in this dialogue is equivalent to 'chaste' or 'virtuous,' it would be superfluous to mention, but that some critics, in their strictness of Hamlet in the present tense, appear to have forgotten it" (217). This is only the first of many times when Hamlet will vent upon Ophelia his disgust at his mother's sexual situation.

We do not learn much about Ophelia during these encounters, but the character of Prince Hamlet becomes clearer each time. Never does he show his cruelty, crudeness, and vulgarity as plainly as when he says, "Get thee to a nunnery" (3.1.120), "That's a fair thought to lie between a maid's legs" (3.2.119), and "It would cost you a groaning to take off mine edge" (3.2.251).

Maynard Mack believes that "nunnery" is used ambiguously and that both interpretations deal with sexuality: "If Ophelia is what she seems, this dirty-minded world of murder, incest, lust, adultery, is no place for her. And if she is not what she seems, then a nunnery in its other sense of 'brothel' is relevant to her" (44).

I tend to believe that either interpretation has more to do with Hamlet and his state of mind than with Ophelia and what she seems or seems not to be. Alexander says that in this scene "Shakespeare makes the hardest demand that any dramatist can make of his principal actor. He asks him to lose the sympathy of the audience" (144). Again, Hamlet's interaction with Ophelia allows the audience to become better acquainted with him and not with her.

Hamlet's words (3.2.119), spoken while he sits beside Ophelia, are so plain that interpretation is unnecessary. "His words are concerned with the act that young lovers usually perform in private. They are of such an unexampled sexual frankness that they have provoked a general reaction of critical shock and an unusual, if uneasy, editorial silence" (Alexander 145).

When Hamlet sits at Ophelia's feet, his words (3.2.251) again reveal his state of mind: "It will cost Ophelia the 'groaning' of losing her virginity to take the 'edge' off his wit or sexual appetite" (Alexander 148).

Rebecca West says that these exchanges between Hamlet and Ophelia are proof that Ophelia was not a chaste young woman.

"That is shown by her tolerance of Hamlet's obscene conversations, which cannot be explained as consistent with the custom of the times" (19).

I maintain that it does more to show Hamlet's obsession with sexual corruption which the Ghost intentionally planted firmly in his son's mind and that we know little more of Ophelia than when the exchanges began.

Alexander says that Ophelia is the most important character in helping to provide a "searching examination of Hamlet's own role in the play." Hamlet sees Ophelia as a threat to "his memory, his dedication, to the task of revenge, and to his whole existence. Only when she is dead does he recognize that this view was wholly and disastrously mistaken" (129).

When next we meet Ophelia (4.5.48-66), she is mad and singing a bawdy song of which Robertson Davies says, "The coarseness…is characteristic of madness. Many people reveal an astonishing knowledge of obscene language…when their wits leave them" (120).

Peter Seng says that the dramatic function of Ophelia's songs is to show more of the character of Hamlet, Laertes, and Polonius, that they sullied her innocence with their cynicism, crudity, and misguided warnings (146-147).

It is not too difficult to read in the words of Ophelia's song the very warnings given her by her father and brother and the same sexual situations that Hamlet spoke to her about. Again, we learn no more of Ophelia except that she is mad.

When next Ophelia appears, she hands out a selection of herbs to Laertes, Claudius, and Gertrude. As we have seen in "A Document in Madness," this is another commentary on characters other than Ophelia. She is still just a mad girl, but through her actions we gain considerable insight into the true characters of Laertes, Claudius, and Gertrude.

Ophelia comes to us next in Gertrude's description of her drowning. This scene is a culmination of all that Ophelia has narrated in the play. A garland of such gross, rank, and vile vegetation cannot be found elsewhere in literature! All of the sexual corruption that lies at the basis of Hamlet is symbolized in the herbs that make up the "fantastic garland" and even in the Willow tree on which the unfortunate Ophelia sought to hang it.

One word Gertrude uses in her description serves as a reaffirmation of the idea of sexual corruption displayed in the garland. "Her clothes spread wide, / and mermaid-like awhile they bore her up" (4.7.175-76). This description of Ophelia as a half-fish, half-woman is very unlikely, or at least, intended as a double entendre. "Mermaid" in the sixteenth and seventeenth centuries was commonly applied to a prostitute (OED).

Her main purpose then, this mystery-girl, was to serve as a vehicle by which Shakespeare could suggest to the audience certain characterizations of Laertes, Claudius, Gertrude, and Hamlet. Nowhere does the information become clearer than when Shakespeare uses Ophelia to translate to the audience in the language of herbs.

Granted, the herbs are ambiguous in their language. While fennel suggests lust, it also means "flattery." While the columbine is the symbol of cuckoldry, it also means "thankless."

It is this tendency toward ambiguity that causes the herbs to fit so very well into Hamlet. Ambiguous words such as honest, liberal, nunnery, mermaid, and loose, add to the idea of sexual corruption because of their ambiguous meanings. Hamlet's relationship with Ophelia is ambiguous. He desires her, but "hates the very desire itself" (Wagner 95). Even the circumstances of Ophelia's death are ambiguous and open to interpretation. The question of suicide or accidental drowning persists (Lyons 62).

There is, however, consistency in the herbs' ambiguities. A connection to things sexual - from the common name of the pansy, "cull-me," meaning "fondle me," to the grossly sexual Arum-Orchis-long purple of Ophelia's fantastic garland - is the common thread that runs through them all.

My intention in this work was to show that Shakespeare wrote for his audience, and that that audience was keenly aware of common lore about the herbs in the play. Without considerable research, we, a twentieth-first century audience, are not even remotely aware of this lore.

However, we do have our counterparts of this symbolic practice. If a comedian walks on stage today and mentions "Spanish Fly," how many in the audience thinks of a European beetle, Lytta vesicatoria?

If that comedian mentions eating lots of oysters, how many sly grins does he draw from the audience? If he simply stands and repeats the word Viagara over and over, does the crowd roar?

These three examples hold for the modern audience much the same associations that I believe the herbs in Hamlet held for Shakespeare's audience.

In the words of Michael MacDonald, the main problem with historical criticism occurs when the researcher offers a "single correct version" of a work of literature instead of "creating new perspectives" on that work (309).

My goal was to use historical criticism to offer a new perspective on the importance of the role of the herbs in Hamlet.

CONCLUSION

In "Modern Treatment of Herbs in Shakespeare," (chapter one), I quoted from Ellacombe's comments on Shakespeare's use of herbs in his works: "When he names a plant or flower, he does so not to show his knowledge, but because the particular flower of plant is wanted in the particular place in which he uses it" (3).

I believe this statement to be true and accurate. This knowledge, or herb-lore, both literary and traditional, was ubiquitous in the Renaissance, and it has not been adequately treated in centuries of criticism of Shakespeare's works. In Hamlet, where even fewer herbs are mentioned than in other plays, the herbs are central to an overwhelming leitmotif of sexual corruption that runs through the entire play.

Hamlet is a giant, unweeded garden where fornication, cuckoldry, incest, lust, and lechery grow rampant and unchecked. Throughout this garden Shakespeare plants herbs in the hands of Ophelia, who passes those herbs along to the appropriate recipients, thereby clarifying and elucidating their characters for the audience.

Johnson (along with other critics) was accurate in his assertion that Ophelia, "the young, the beautiful, the harmless, and the pious" (Wagner 96), is an important character. I also believe her to be absolutely essential to the play, but in an oblique way. I have shown that Ophelia's importance lies in her position as a messenger from the playwright to the audience. Interesting, and worthy of further examination, is Shakespeare's choosing this relatively innocent and trusting girl to play the part of a harbinger of sexual tidings.

BIBLIOGRAPHY

Alexander, Nigel. Poison, Play, and Duel. Lincoln: U of Nebraska P., 1971.

Anderson, Frank J.   An Illustrated History of the Herbals. New York: Columbia UP, 1977.

Arber, Agnes. Herbals: Their Origin and History: A Chapter in the History of Botany, 1470-1670. London: Cambridge UP, 1953.

Banckes, Rycharde. An Herbal.   Facsimile of 1525 London edition. Eds. Sanford Larkey and Thomas Pyle. New York: Scholars Facsimile, 1941.

Beisley, Sidney.   Shakspere's   Garden.   London: Longman's, 1864.

Bloom, J. Harvey.   Shakespeare's Garden.   London: Metheun, 1903.

Bradley, Henry.   "'Cursed Hebenon' (or 'Hebona')." Modern Language Review. 15 (1920); 85-87.

Browning, Robert.   Paracelsus (1835).   London: Oxford UP, 1983. Vol. 1 of The Poetical Works of Robert Browning. 2 vols.

Bunney, Sarah. The Illustrated Book of Herbs: Their Medicinal and Culinary uses. New York: Gallery Books, 1984.

Butler, Samuel. Hudibras. (1663). Ed. John Wilders. Oxford: Clarendon, 1967.

Campion, Thomas. Campion's Works. Ed. Percival Vivian. Oxford, Clarendon, 1909.

Chaucer, Geoffrey. "The legend of Good Women." The Riverside Chaucer. Gen. Ed. Larry D. Benson. 3rd ed. Boston: Houghton, 1987.

Coats, Alice. Flowers and their Histories. New York: Pitman, 1956.

Culpeper, Nicholas. Culpeper's Complete Herbal. London: [n.p.], 1653.

Davies, Robertson. Shakespeare's Boy Actors. London: J.M. Dent, 1939.

Dent, Allen. The World of Shakespeare. New York: Taplinger, 1974.

Dioscorides, Pedacious. Materia Medica. c. AD 50. Rpt. as The Greek Herbal of Dioscorides. Ed. Robert Gunther. (1933). New York: Hafner, 1959.

Erier, Catriona Tudor. "Parsley, Sage, Rosemary, and Thyme." The Christian Science Monitor. 18 May 1988: 23-24.

Durant, Will, and Ariel Durant. The Life of Greece. New York: Simon, 1966. Volume 2 of The Story of Civilization. 11 vols. 1935-1975.

Edwards, John., ed. and trans. The Roman Cookery of Apicius. De Re Coquinaria. [c. Ad 450]. Washington: Hartley & Marks, 1984.

Eliade, Mercia. Patterns in Comparative Religion. Trans. Rosemary Sheed. New York, New American Library, 1984.

Ellacombe, Rev. Henry N. The Plant Lore and Garden Craft of Shakespeare. Exeter: [n.p.], 1878.

Furness, Horace Howard, ed. Hamlet. By William Shakespeare. New York: American Scholar, 1965. Vol. 1 of The New Variorum Shakespeare.

Gerard, John. Gerard's Herball. Ed. Thomas Johnston (1636). New York: Crescent Books, 1985.

Grieve, Maude. A Modern Herbal. (1931). 2 Vols. Ed. Mrs. C.F. Leyel. New York: Hafner, 1967.

Griggs, Barbara. Green Pharmacy: A History of Herbal Medicine. London: Robert Hale, 1987.

Grigson, Geoffrey. The Englishman's Flora. Manchester: [n.p.], 1883.

Harbage, Alfred. Shakespeare's Audience. New York: Columbia UP, 1958.

Hazlitt, William. (1776-1830). The Roundtable: The Characters of Shakespeare's Plays. New York: Dutton, 1951.

Hoeniger, F.D., and J.F.M. Hoeniger. The Development of Natural History In Tudor England. Charlottesville: U of Virginia P, 1973.

Holland, Philemon, trans. The Natural History. By C. Plinius Secundus (c. AD 65). Ed. Paul Turner. New York: McGraw-Hill, 1964.

Horn, Walter, and Ernest Born. The Plan of St. Gall: A study of the Architecture and Economy of, and Life in a Paradigmatic Carolingian Monastery. Berkley: U of California P, 1979.

Jenkins, Harold, ed. The Arden Shakespeare Hamlet. New York: Metheun, 1982.

Kowalchic, Claire, and William Hylton., eds. Rodale's illustrated Encyclopedia of Herbs. Emmaus, Pennsylvania: Rodale Press, 1987.

Krutch, Joseph Wood. The Gardener's World. New York: Putnam, 1959.

Laufer, Geraldine, Adamich. "Shakespeare's Herbs: Fertile Subjects for the Garden." Southern Accents July-Aug. 1988: 20-26.

Lyte, Henry. Nievve Herball, or Historie of Plants (1578). London: Edward Griffen, 1619.

MacDonald, Michael. "Ophelia's Maimed Rites." Shakespeare Quarterly 36 (1986): 309-317.

Maplet, John. A Greene Forest (1567). London: Hesperides, 1930.

Markham, Gervase. The English Housewife (1615). Ed. Michael r. Best. Montreal: McGill-Queen's UP, 1986.

Marlowe, Christopher. The Jew of Malta (1633). The Complete Works of Christopher Marlowe. Ed. Fredson Bowers. London: Cambridge UP, 1973.

Marvell, Andrew. "The Mower Against Gardens" (1681). The Poetry of Andrew Marvell. Ed. Dennis Davison. London: Edward Arnold, 1964.

McCann, Justin, trans. The Rule of St. Benedict (c. AD 500). London: Sheed & Ward, 1976.

Morris, Harry. "Ophelia's 'Bonnie Sweet Robin.'" PMLA 73 (1958): 601-603.

Oxford English Dictionary. Eds. Dr. C.T. Onions and Sir William Craigie. London: Oxford UP, 1971.

Otten, Charlotte. Environ'd With Eternity: God, Poems, and Plants in Sixteenth and Seventeenth Century England. Kansas: Coronado Press, 1985.

---. "Ophelia's 'Long Purples' or 'Dead Men's Fingers.'" Shakespeare Quarterly 30 (1979): 397-402.

Parkinson, John. Paridisi In Sole Paradisus Terrestrus (1629). Norwood, J. J.: Walter Johnson, 1975.

Partridge, Eric. Origins: A Short Etymological Dictionary of Modern English. New York: Greenwich House, 1983.

---. Shakespeare's Bawdy. New York: E.P.Dutton, 1960.

Rowse, A.L. The Annotated Shakespeare. By William Shakespeare. New York: Greenwich House, 1988.

Seager, H.W. Natural History in Shakespeare's Time. London [n.p.], 1896.

Shakespeare, William. The Riverside Shakespeare. Ed. G. Blakemore Evans. Boston: Houghton Mifflin, 1974.

Singer, Charles. From Magic To Science. London: Ernest Benn, 1921.

Singleton, Esther. The Shakespeare Garden. London: Metheun, 1932.

Soleki, Ralph S. "Shanidar IV, a Neanderthal Flower Burial in Northern Iraq." SCIENCE 190 (1975): 880-881.

Spenser, Edmund. The Faerie Queen. (1589). The Poetical Works. Eds. J.C. Smith and E. De Salencourt. London: Oxford UP, 1912.

Spurgeon, Caroline. Shakespeare's Imagery. Boston: Beacon, 1961.

Staunton, Howard, ed. The Works of Shakespeare. By William Shakespeare. London: Rutledge & Sons, 1866.

Tergit, Gabriele. Flowers Through The Ages. London: Oswald Wolff, 1961.

Thiselton-Dyer, T.F. Folklore of Shakespeare. New York: Harper, 1884.

---. The Folklore of Plants. London: [n.p.], 1889.

Turner, William. A New Herbal. Collen, England: [n.p.], 1568.

Wagner, Linda Weshimer. "Ophelia: Shakespeare's Pathetic Plot Device." Shakespeare Quarterly 14 (1965): 94-97.

Warburton, William, editor of complete works of William Shakespeare, 1747. As quoted in Notes & Queries 7 (1883): 193.

Wentersdorf, Karl P. "Hamlet: Ophelia's Long Purples." Shakespeare Quarterly 29 (1978): 413-417.

West, Rebecca. The Court and the Castle. New Haven: Yale UP, 1957.

Wilson, Dover. What Happens In Hamlet. London: Cambridge UP, 1970.

Wither, George. "Britains Remembrancer."   (1628). As quoted in Notes & Queries 7 (1883): 193.

Wright, L.B. Middle-Class Culture in Elizabethan England. Chapel Hill: U of North Carolina P, 1935.

ABOUT THE AUTHOR:

Annis Ward Jackson grew up in the Appalachian Mountains of North Carolina where two branches of her family have lived for nine generations and where storytelling has been a pastime for hundreds of years.

Writing in some form for most of her life, her goal has been to entertain her readers with some stories and inform them with others.

Jackson earned an MA at East Carolina University in Greenville, NC and taught English at Barton College in Wilson, NC. Before returning to the mountains in 1993, she was an English as a Second Language Special Project Director for the NC Department of Community Colleges.

Jackson is an intensive gardener and horsewoman. Both subjects appear frequently in her writing. She lives in the North Carolina mountains with her husband, Kramer, their standard poodles, Daisy and Sophie, and quarter horses, Brick and Sunny.

Printed in Great Britain
by Amazon

52795211R00058